Our children no longer believe in the old adage, 'Children are to be seen and not heard.' I can't imagine Kimberly making such a statement! If she would have, this book would be full of blank pages. In fact, she acted on the contrary, and I'm so glad she did! In her book, *Out of the Mouths of Babes: Daily Devotions from Our Greatest Teachers*, Kimberly wrote whatever came out of her children's mouth and began to tie their sayings into biblical and spiritual truths. Be prepared to be transformed!

—LaMarr Darnell Shields, Ed.M.
President, Urban Leadership Institute
Author, *10 Steps Out of Puberty:
A Teen's Guide to Successful Living*
www.urbanleadershipinstitute.com

Out of the Mouths of Babes: Daily Devotions from Our Greatest Teachers is truly Cosbyesque, full of wit and wisdom. The lessons here we will all remember from Sunday school. And the message in Parker's fine testament to ageless truth is quite simple: listen and learn.

—Kwame Alexander
Author and Producer of the Capital BookFest
www.capitalbookfest.org

Out of the Mouths of Babes: Daily Devotions from Our Greatest Teachers is a read I recommend for all parents. The book's content spoke to me personally as a wife, mother, and entrepreneur. One of my main goals as a mother of three is to instill lasting values and principles in my children and this book promotes just that. The true life experiences shared by the author add an appealing authenticity to the book's pages. I was especially drawn to the candor of the book as the author emphasized the need for parents to always say what needs to be said with assurance; therefore, remaining true to ourselves and trustworthy to others. Moreover, the book offers a special appeal as the author includes a page after each entry to allow moms like me to write down my own thoughts and feelings. This book is certainly a MUST READ."

—Cheryl M. Wood
Owner
Moms R The Best
www.momsrthebest.com

OUT OF THE MOUTHS
OF BABES

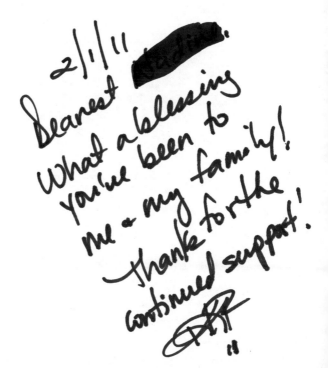

OUT OF THE MOUTHS
OF BABES

**Daily Devotions from
Our Greatest Teachers**

KIMBERLY K. PARKER

TATE PUBLISHING *& Enterprises*

The opinions expressed by the author are not necessarily those of Tate Publishing, LLC.

Published by Tate Publishing & Enterprises, LLC
127 E. Trade Center Terrace | Mustang, Oklahoma 73064 USA
1.888.361.9473 | www.tatepublishing.com

Tate Publishing is committed to excellence in the publishing industry. The company reflects the philosophy established by the founders, based on Psalm 68:11,
"The Lord gave the word and great was the company of those who published it."

Published in the United States of America

ISBN: 978-1-61739-316-7
1. Religion: Christian Life: Inspirational
2. Religion: Christian Life: Family
10.12.10

Dedication

In loving memory of the matriarchs who profoundly impacted my life: my maternal great-grandmother, Roberta "Boy" Hill Smith; my paternal grandmother, Olivia "Mittis" DeBraux; and my mother, Barbara "Bobbie" Lee Hill DeBraux. Continue to surround me with your spirits.

Acknowledgments

To my heavenly Father, the Son, and the Holy Spirit. I reverently honor you. Whenever I've called, you've answered. Whenever one tear began to fall, you told me, "It is well." Whenever the trying days and even more trying nights appeared to never end, you reiterated your plan for my life and gave me reasons to press on. I am because you are the great I AM. I live because you are the Living Word. Thank you for being my source. Thank you for all the many blessings you continuously bestow upon me and my family. You have been extremely kind and most generous with your love.

To my husband and brother in Christ, Kenneth A. Parker. Truly, we serve a faithful God. You are so dear to me. Your priceless love and support are always backed by your actions. The respect I have for you runs deeper than any well. Thank you for your endearing spiritual leadership. Thank you for being a true man of God. Thank you for going above and beyond the call of every duty to ensure your family's protection. Thank you for allowing me to maximize my role as your wife and the mother of our children. Indeed, you are second to none; and I am better than blessed to have you as mine.

To my four beautiful children: Bricen Anthony, Khalil DeBraux, Kalonji Ameer, and Kalani Kay. You are the pulse of my heart. I am so honored to be the one God saw fit to train you. I love and appreciate each of you and am grateful that you are truly God's finest. I pray that you know that I have your best interests at heart. Humbly, I ask that you forgive me for any mistakes I make along the way.

To my pastor, Reverend Damion M. Briggs. Your teachings continue to take me to greater dimensions in my relationship with God. Thank you for imparting the Word so powerfully and telling it like it is. The Word of God is indeed sharper than any two-edged sword. God has used you to help carve me into a new creature.

To Kwame Alexander, LaMarr Darnell Shields, Rhonda C. Keith, and Cheryl Wood. Thank you for making time to render your thoughts on this book. I appreciate your honest feedback and support.

Table of Contents

Foreword

Many of us have inherited the philosophy that children should be seen and not heard. This thought is an outgrowth of the Apostle Paul's statement, "Women should keep silent in the church," (1 Corinthians 14:34, NIV). I believe that adults who maintain this level of thinking do so in an effort to shield themselves from the truth that children so freely express. Oftentimes, the things that children utter come to challenge and even convict us because what we say and do are in direct opposition to one another. We must really ask ourselves where we would be as a community, nation, and as a society if children were not allowed to express themselves.

Out of the Mouths of Babes: Daily Devotions from Our Greatest Teachers is an attempt to amplify the still, small voices of an often-neglected source of pride, strength, courage, inspiration, and even wisdom: children. Children are a true blessing from God and deserve to be seen, heard, and listened to. This book serves as a reminder of the profound practical and spiritual benefits of giving voice to our most prized possessions.

The value of children in our society and our ability to accept them as intellectual beings has more to do with our will than their skill. The mere thought of silencing children infuriates me as an educator and parent. An experience that confirmed for me why it is essential that children are both seen and heard came as a result of a statement made by my eleven-year-old son, Khalil. He was so impressed with then-Senator Barack Obama during the 2008 presidential debate that he stated, "I want to meet him someday." Rather than dismissing what he uttered, my wife and I affirmed his vision; and one year following his inauguration, we found ourselves greeted by President Barack Obama in the Oval Office as a result of a personal invitation.

Out of the Mouths of Babes: Daily Devotions from Our Greatest Teachers contains merely a smidgeon of the wonderful lessons that have been gleaned from these children. We are indeed indebted to those people—like my lovely wife, Kimberly K. Parker—who humble themselves long enough to give life to the words that children speak.

Proverbs 23:7 declares, "As a man thinketh so is he," (NIV). These words are life-giving and life-changing and have the ability to bring into existence whatsoever we truly believe. Therefore, let us not minimize or underscore the ability of children to teach us truths.

—Rev. Kenneth A. Parker, EdM

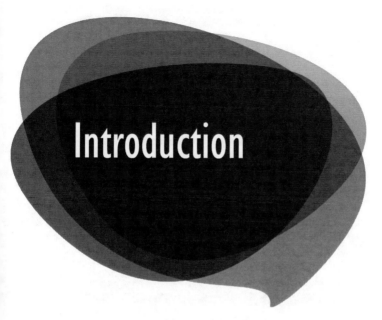

Introduction

In the 1990's, Bill Cosby hosted a very popular American television show called *Kids Say the Darndest Things.* The premise of the show was that the host would ask a question to a child around the age of three to eight, who would usually respond in a "cute" way.[1] I remember all too well how glued to the tube I used to be when the show was airing. After a long day of work and attending classes, I looked forward to the stress-busting wit of those children. Easily humored, a sore stomach was my reward after hearing the tales they uttered. I remember one particular show when a child was asked the age of his mother. The child replied most sincerely, "Oh, she's about the same age as God." I can still see the stunned look on that mother's face.

Not long after the show aired, I conceived a child of my own. God spoke clearly to Kenny and said, "You will call him 'Khalil.'" I will never forget how thrilled we were. Our family and friends shared our joy and exclaimed excitement about Khalil as well. We took great pride in recapping the story of how God gave our son his name. But more than a name, he gave us to know what he was going to be: a boy.

Khalil (meaning "sincere friend") DeBraux Parker spoke his first identifiable word on June 25, 1999 at eight months old. I had assumed my first position as a praise dance instructor for a local church's summer camp and left him to be cared for by someone else for the first time in four months. Upon arriving to retrieve him, he looked at me with the most gorgeous smile and said, "Hi." I was so tickled. After that, his vocabulary developed rather quickly. I can clearly recall being greeted every morning with, "Where's my dada?" as my child stood in the far-left corner of his crib. Kenny and I minimized baby talk with Khalil and we made sure that those who communicated with him obliged. *Bottle* is pronounced "bot-tle" (bawt-l), not "ba-ba."

When Khalil was two, I began to listen intuitively to what he expressed and how it applied to my life. It was as if God was saying, "See, Kimberly. This is what I have been trying to tell you." The first occurrence was profoundly applicable to my current state of affairs. Immediately, I sent out an e-mail to a few friends, and this is what I shared:

> Khalil, who turned two on 10/20/00, has been potty trained since 12/10/00. While this is still new to him, I constantly ask, "Noodle, do you have to go potty?" Of course, he tells me, "No." However, I generally take him to the potty, and he generally goes.
>
> One day while we were playing, he said, "Momma, you go potty?" I did what he does and said, "No." With such encouragement, he replied, "It's easy, Momma!" After I laughed, I remembered that God said, "It's easy," too. He said, "For my yoke is easy, and my burden is light." Sounds good to me.

Whatever your situation may be on this day, remember that this is what God said in Matthew 11:30.

The response to that e-mail was overwhelming. Many replied with, "Thank you, Sister Parker. I needed to hear that." What they did not know is that I said the same thing to Khalil. It was a most humbling experience to see how those three simple words out of the mouth of my two-year-old impacted my life and the lives of so many others.

From that point on, hearing Khalil took on a whole new meaning. I could not believe what was happening. The more he talked, the more spiritual insight I gained. Even when I tried to dismiss the revelation as "cute" or "He is just two," God continued to say, "Listen." Not only did I listen, but I began to take notes (on whatever little piece of paper I could find) and compiled his gems of wisdom.

It would not be long before I realized that God was preparing me to write this book. I truly believe that everything begins with a thought. So I began to visualize my book, developed the title, and listed those persons whose assistance I would solicit. I mentioned my vision to no one but my husband, and as always, he encouraged me to pursue my dreams.

Doubt attempted to cloud my vision. Yet, the mere thought of abandoning this project was met head-on with confirmation from someone or something that writing a book is exactly what I should pursue. On one occasion, I shared more of what Khalil said with my girlfriend Rhonda. After we laughed a bit and echoed how cute he was, she said, "Chil', you need to write a book. That Khalil is something."

I simply replied, "I am."

Over the course of three years, I had logged over a hundred of Khalil's timely revelations. After my second child, Kalonji Ameer (meaning "victorious prince") Parker, began to talk, the documentation continued. Although I was prepared to begin, taking the first step was very difficult. Then it happened. One morning, while communing with God, I began rereading *Tapping the Power Within: A Path to Self-empowerment for Black Women* by Iyanla Vanzant. This is what she said:

> Spiritually, we are all teachers and students at the same time ... Spiritually, in any life experi-

ence, we are either learning a lesson, teaching the lesson or the object by which the lesson will be taught. Once we understand our role, we know our task. When we know our task, the lesson and the reward come quickly and easily… Spiritual teachers realize that everything we think, do and say will return to us in the mirror of self when the spirit is ready to learn the lesson. A spiritual teacher is also the individual who shares spiritual knowledge with you and assists you on your path to spiritual realization. Often, this can be done without knowledge on the part of either party. The key is to realize, whoever assists you in becoming a better, more enlightened individual is a spiritual teacher. For adults, our greatest spiritual teachers are our children.[2]

In this second edition, I attempt to spread the healing, enlightenment, and growth afforded me through my sons and now my daughter, Kalani Kay (meaning "the heavens rejoice") Parker, or "Lady," as she is affectionately called. I also provided ample space for you to journal your experiences as you read this book. I am a firm believer that writing renews the mind and liberates the soul.

I pray that God will open your heart and mind to glean from my children's innocence and yield to their advice. I caution you not to second guess their ability, through the wise counsel of the Holy Spirit, to help you as well. I guarantee that your life will never be the same again.

> Out of the mouth of babes and sucklings hast thou ordained strength because of thine enemies, that thou mightest still the enemy and the avenger.
>
> Psalm 8:2 (KJV)

A Letter to My Children

My beloved Khalil, Kalonji, and Kalani,

Opportunity, op· por· tu· ni· ty (op-er-too-ni-tee): a situation or condition favorable for attainment of a goal.

Of all the words *Webster's Dictionary* contains, this is the word that best describes *Out of the Mouths of Babes: Daily Devotions from Our Greatest Teachers.* Herein is the chance, the most favorable circumstance, to transfer to our readers a toolbox that will aid them as they hammer out hope, measure every milestone, and pave a path to their purpose.

When I finally began writing this book, I had only one hope in mind: to share with others how the three of you have helped me grow spiritually. Driven solely by my love for you, dreams of fortune, fame, and potential accolades from readers mattered not. I merely want you and those who have the pleasure of meeting you through these pages to know that your momma adores you so much that she would take the time to write about you and the life-transforming power of your innocent words.

Sweethearts, my encounters with you have given me the courage to share very personal pieces of my life. There is profound liberation that engulfs me as a result of being so transparent. I believe with all my heart that my unabashed example will permit our readers to face their issues head-on, turn to God in prayer, surrender to the guidance of the Holy Spirit, and begin to walk in liberty. What a powerful experience.

To you, Khalil, Kalonji, and Kalani, I render my most sincere gratitude for giving me amazing joy. Truly, I am abundantly blessed to have you as my children. Khalil, when you tell me, "Momma, you are *so* beautiful," know that you radiate likewise. Kalonji, when you tell me, "Momma, I am so proud of you," know that I am even more proud of you. Kalani, when you tell me, "Momma, I just love you," always know that I will forever love you too.

Forever appreciative and most humbled,

—*Momma*

Something Happened

Proudly, I attest to keeping my hair healthy, neat, and presentable. Whether I sport cornrows, an Afro, two-strand twists, or a press-and-curl, my tresses radiate beautifully. Occasionally, when I find that I am in-between hair styles, I will adorn my head with an African wrap. Even then, my crown draws attention.

During one of my in-between moments, Khalil encountered my hair unwrapped. It was sitting high upon my head in its most natural state, free to be what God created it to be. Albeit a bit untamed, this was not the first time he noticed my crown in such a manner. As he scanned the sight of my hair in all geographical directions, he displayed quite an analytical expression on his beautiful, brown face. I could tell that he was weighing his words carefully as he prepared to speak. Not even a moment later, Khalil ingenuously stated, "Something happened, Momma."

"Something happened." At the utterance of those words, the rewind button of my life stopped on Sunday, April 5, 2009. My spirit was extremely hampered that day at Eastern Community Church.[3] Like an eighteen-wheeler not allowed departure from its dock, I was weighed down beyond capacity and desperate for a serious metamorphosis to occur in my life. I knew that if I continued down the path laden with bitterness, anger, and lack of self-control, I was bound to reach a state of collapse. In other words, I would have destroyed myself and, quite possibly, my family and friends as well.

Throughout the entire service, the Holy Spirit spoke to me. Simply, he stated, "You have a choice to make." I knew exactly what he meant, and I also knew that pending choice was a matter of life or death. I had gotten tired of myself and the way I was acting. Rage would consume me whenever I was challenged in my ability to control certain states of affairs or when a situation mirrored my past. I considered the impact I was having on my children who, more than any other group of persons, witnessed this side of me. I thought, *What am I doing to them?*

Once the service concluded, the invitation was extended to anyone who wanted to become a member of the church. Without delay, a few people made their way toward Pastor Briggs and took a seat on the front pew. I could sense that their load seemed to lighten just by them taking what I am sure felt like a very long walk. Just when I thought it was over, another invitation had been extended. This invitation was for anyone who had already accepted Christ in their life, yet their relationship with Christ was being hindered. He went on to say that, for such persons, there was neither any sign of growth nor fruit-bearing because the act of surrendering their life to Christ had not occurred. What an epiphanic moment. The only component missing from this invitation was a huge sign that read, "See Kimberly Kay Parker."

The mental picture of walking down the aisle was not clear enough to propel action. I stayed seated and began "throwing fleece" just like Gideon.[4] *God, if you really want me to go down there, have him call me by my first, middle, and last name,* I deliberated. Right back at me, the Holy Spirit said, "You know what is in your heart. You have a choice to make."

For a moment longer, I did not move. I could not move. The church was filled to capacity with members and visitors. Generally, I take a seat on that front row as a sign of support to others, not as one who needs support. What would the church think about me, you know, the preacher's wife who dances under such a mighty anointing? More importantly, what would my husband think? Would he be embarrassed? Would he even acknowledge and celebrate my cry out for help? Once again, I heard the Holy Spirit say, "They don't matter. You have a choice to make." Tearfully, I gently whispered, "Help me, please." Not even a second later, I felt my legs standing and my body gliding to the front of the church. There at the altar, I surrendered my life to Christ.

Since that day, my life has changed in so many beautiful ways. While I have moments of relapse, I am equipped now more than ever with the power of God to make necessary changes swiftly. I truly hunger for and take time to study the Word of God. I can audibly hear his voice. My encounters with him are much more frequent. Through his power and love and my ongoing self-inventory, I am taking great strides to chip away at those hardened areas of my life. I've learned to honor my feelings and communicate them as necessary. As I study his Word and sit under sound teachings, the root of my issues is being exposed. I am stronger, wiser, and much bolder than I have ever been in my entire life.

The true and all-wise God is determined to help me become the unwavering woman he created me to be by any means necessary. I am learning to seek the guidance and direction of the Holy Spirit no matter how minute the undertaking. While I have certainly come a long way, I have a long way to go. However, knowing that God has outfitted me with his power to continuously transform my life makes all the difference in the world.

> For ye were as sheep going astray; but are now returned unto the Shepherd and Bishop of your souls.
>
> 1 Peter 2:25 (KJV)

> I am the vine, ye [are] the branches: He that abideth in me, and I in him, the same bringeth forth much fruit: for without me ye can do nothing.
>
> John 15:5 (KJV)

After reading this timeless truth, share something that happened causing you to surrender your life to Christ.

Out of the Mouths of Babes

_____

_____

_____

_____

_____

_____

_____

_____

_____

_____

_____

_____

_____

_____

_____

_____

But You're Good

Khalil excitedly made his way into my bedroom to confirm what he already knew: the laundry was folded and stored and now I was free to play with him. Into my room he trod with a wide grin and said, "Come on, Momma. It's time to color. You can use your favorite color, black, if you want." After finding the most suitable spot on the floor, Khalil pulled out all his books and crayons and the fun began.

Khalil and I colored nearly twelve pages nonstop. While I strongly advocate the incorporation of art into a child's life, I had pretty much reached my limit. The colors started playing tricks with my eyes, thus causing me to go outside the lines. Without warning, I began boxing the crayons I was using and closing the books. Khalil noticed.

"What's wrong, Momma? Don't you like to color?" Khalil asked.

"I love to color. Look at all the pages we did. Momma's just a bit tired and I want to rest my eyes," I said.

"But you're good, Momma. Can't your eyes rest tomorrow?" Khalil inquired.

"Well, Khalil, I … guess they can," I confirmed.

"Good. You want me to get your black crayon for you?" Khalil asked.

As Khalil handed me the crayon, I began thinking of the importance of what transpired. Khalil did not focus on his desire for me to color with him. He did not selfishly perform a whining cry through song and dance. Instead, Khalil sincerely saw my gift of coloring and encouraged me to continue. He noticed that I was good at something that, if shared, could make someone else feel good. Khalil believed in me and what I had to offer and inspired me not to quit.

Oftentimes, we become so consumed with what we are feeling. Being burdened, overwhelmed, depressed, and just outright tired overshadows our ability to glimpse the beauty all around us. Well, today, I want you to take the focus off of yourself. That's right. Shift the microscope such that it centers on someone else. Tell your wife that you appreciate all the love and support she gives. Express yourself by letting your parents know that, in spite of the challenges, they did an exceptional job raising you and your siblings. Impress upon your employees how invaluable their service and commitment are to the company. Take the time to tell somebody something good.

But encourage one another day after day, as
long as it is (still) called "Today."

Hebrews 3:13b (NASB)

After reading this timeless truth, do you know someone who needs encouraging? What are you going to
do to shift the focus off of you and onto her/him?

_____

_____

_____

_____

_____

_____

_____

_____

_____

_____

_____

_____

_____

_____

Don't Leave Me

My trip to the supermarket was long overdue. The refrigerator serenaded me with the echo of my voice, and every single cupboard was nearly bare. One diversion after another twice prevented me from enjoying my bi-weekly rendezvous with the produce aisle, and I could not put it off any longer. It is my preference to go solo between 5:30 a.m. and 6:30 a.m. However, on this particular day, I arrived close to 10:00 a.m. and had both Khalil and Kalonji with me. *Oh joy,* I thought sarcastically.

Contrary to my anticipation, it was not nearly as adventurous as it could have been. Khalil and Kalonji occupied each other quite well for the hour and half we were there. They kept their little hands off of the shelves, not once rolled over the back of my foot with the cart, and even accepted every, "No," in response to their request for those tasty-looking snacks with first, middle, and last name ingredients. *What is sodium stearoyl lactylate exactly*, I wondered. When it was time to check out, they graciously helped by throwing my items on the conveyor, bread and eggs first, of course. I really do not know how I would have managed without them.

With bags and children loaded into the truck, I made my way home. I was certain that the ride home would lull the boys to sleep, considering all the energy they exerted at the supermarket. Upon arriving, I immediately began to unload the endless rows of bags. Unsurprisingly, Kalonji was wide-awake and still full of energy. Customarily, he jumped right in and began helping me. Khalil, on the other hand, had drifted off to sleep of course. Startled by all the movement and noise coming from the bags, he jumped up; reached his hands for me; and desperately cried, "Don't leave me, Momma." My heartstrings were pulled like never before. I felt his woe ever so deeply within. His beautiful, brown eyes swelled with tears and his hands began to shake. In my best reassuring tone, I gently cupped his chubby cheeks, hugged him just tight enough to assure him of my presence, and said, "Khalil, I will never leave you." I sat and held him for a while. I wanted him to not only hear my words but to see and feel the action behind those words. Once he regained a sense of where he was, he hugged me back and shook his head affirmatively. Then he made his way into the house, and I continued unloading the groceries.

Have you ever been left—left behind, left out, or left to your own devices? I have on more than a few occasions. Never to welcome such with open arms, I found myself alone, afraid, and even ashamed. However, it's reassuring to know that God never leaves us. Never. Allow me to highlight a few of the countless examples of God remaining with His people:

> He was with Esther as she entered King Xerxes's chambers without invitation (Esther 5).
>
> He was with Jonah in the fish's belly (Jonah 2).
>
> He was with David while battling Goliath (1 Samuel 17).
>
> He was with Elijah in the wilderness (1 Kings 19).
>
> He was with me while engulfed in a deep state of depression in 2002.

Regardless of our predicaments, God never left any of us. Never. By the way, just in case you are wondering, he will never leave you either.

> Be strong and of good courage, fear not, nor be afraid of them: for the Lord thy God, he it

is that doth go with thee; he will not fail thee, nor forsake thee.

Deuteronomy 31:6 (KJV)

And these three men, Shadrach, Meshach, and Abednego, fell down bound into the midst of the burning fiery furnace. He answered and said, Lo, I see four men loose, walking in the midst of the fire, and they have no hurt; and the form of the fourth is like the Son of God.

Daniel 3:23, 25

After reading this timeless truth, are you feeling alone, afraid, or even ashamed? You do not have to stay this way because God is right there with you. Use these lines to talk to God and then pray that God will send a trustworthy person your way to talk to as well.

_____

_____

_____

_____

_____

_____

_____

_____

_____

_____

_____

_____

_____

_____

_____

A Piece Is Missing

The best gift one could ever buy for Khalil is a puzzle. He utterly enjoys breaking them into their many pieces and putting them back together again. Quite an analytical child, he has also taken a liking to crossword puzzles, mazes, memory games, and word find activities as well. If, due to a bad dream, Khalil has risen a little earlier than usual, he will retrieve one of those pastimes and opt to not go back to sleep. What a smart way to keep his mind off of the fiend that visited him.

I am extremely honored that Khalil delights in playing with me. Generally, he extends an invitation to join him and I most gladly accept. On one particular occasion, we were doing his choice dinosaur puzzle when an amazing discovery took place: a piece was missing. Khalil gasped deeply. Taking my cue, I immediately began to search for the missing piece. There alongside me was Khalil, pursuing in like manner. To our dismay, we could not find the one missing piece that would make this puzzle complete.

The "start-to-finish" type A personalities that we are, I saw just how emotionally invested Khalil and I were both becoming. We had to find that missing piece now. Slightly dismayed, I suggested to Khalil that we take a break and look for it later. As we shifted our attention to watching television, I began to reminisce. Almost immediately, my mind took me back to a time in my life when, like that puzzle, a piece was missing.

It certainly has been a while since I put pen to paper. Lord knows I don't mean to ignore you like this, but you're a journal...not a diary. There have just been so many changes in my life and they have kept me so busy. I's married now! Yep! Said, "I do" to that handsome Country-boy named Kenneth Anthony Parker. Fine as May wine! Who would have thought that walking into that restaurant in Norfolk and meeting him would produce all this? He's a good man. Can't wait until he comes back from Houston. Sure do miss him. Taking a break from school this summer. Gotta prepare to move and stuff. Work is going well. Just earned another raise. 'Bout time they recognized my contributions to that company! Shucks, with all the "beyond-the-call-of-duty" tasks I undertake my picture should be on the wall (ha, ha, ha). Octavia still does her thang. She gets me from point A to point B with no problem. It's a wonder the owner ever sold her. In a nutshell, all is so well. I feel great, look marvelous (went from a plump size 16 to a pleasant size eight), got money, and married to the best thang since vanilla ice cream. But, something is missing. I mean, with all that I have, I just ain't right. I don't feel complete. I know what it is and have known for a long time: I need Jesus! Of this one thing I'm sure. I've put Him off far too long. Hope it's not too late. Gonna call Lauren and see if I can go to church with her on Sunday. I'm sure she won't mind … [v]

After I spoke to Lauren, I got on my knees and prayed. I cried uncontrollably for a very long time as I apologized to God profusely. I had so many blessings in my life, but I was not honoring the Blessed One with my life. I wondered, *What a friend we have in Jesus, but what kind of friend am I being to him?*[6] I asked the Lord to forgive me, come back into my life, and teach me how to live for him. The following Sunday, while at church with Lauren, I anxiously anticipated the call to discipleship. Once the doors of the church were opened, I publicly rededicated my life to Christ.

The missing piece of the puzzle of my life was found; and at once, I felt complete.

At the conclusion of the television program, Khalil announced that our break was over. As we resumed our search, we found that missing puzzle piece in no time at all. Beaming with pride, Khalil handed it to me and said, "Momma, you do it." "It would be my pleasure, Khalil," I replied. Just as I did in 1994, I placed the missing piece where it belonged and the puzzle was complete.

> And ye are complete in him, which is the head of all principality and power:
>
> Colossians 2:10 (KJV)

> … and you have a full and true life in Christ, who is ruler over all rulers and powers.
>
> Colossians 2:10 (NCV)

> You don't need a telescope, a microscope, or a horoscope to realize the fullness of Christ, and the emptiness of the universe without him. When you come to him, that fullness comes together for you, too. His power extends over everything.
>
> Colossians 2:10 (MSG)

After reading this timeless truth, is your life incomplete? Is there something missing? Use these lines to talk to God and pray for the assistance of the Holy Spirit as you become complete in him.

_____

_____

_____

_____

_____

_____

_____

_____

_____

_____

_____

_____

_____

_____

_____

Food, Shelter, Clothing, and Entertainment

Khalil and I found ourselves alone in my bedroom. The rest of the family decided on a television show while snacking on popcorn in the kitchen. As he shifted from one end to the other in search of the ultimate spot on my bed, I could sense that Khalil wanted to ask something of me. Mothers just know their children. Moments later, Khalil hesitantly asked about a toy he wanted to order online.

"Momma, um, there is something that I just gotta have," he presented.

"Oh, is that right?" I inquired.

"Yes. I think I'm the only one in my class who does not have this one," he continued.

"Well, Khalil, it's okay to be the only one in certain situations. It sets you apart from the crowd," I said in my most convincing tone.

"This is different, Momma. I need this toy. For real," he stated emphatically.

"Khalil, the only thing you need is food, shelter, and clothing," I retorted.

"And entertainment," he countered.

Imagine, if you will, the rolling over with laughter that ensued immediately thereafter. I was extremely weak in the knees after hearing that yet another essential element to maintaining life, according to my son, was the need to be entertained. In my motion-picture mind, I envisioned Khalil gasping for air after winning a marathon and instead of asking for water he asked, dryly, "Please, Momma, give me some entertainment." You gotta love children.

Khalil, like you and I, often confuse our needs with our wants. We need to consume vitamins, proteins, and minerals in order to survive; but we want to eat ice cream, candy, and chips from time to time. We need shelter to protect our bodies from the elements, but we want a house with a three-car garage. We need to be covered with clothing for reasons too numerous to name, but we want garments that are designed by the latest fashion gurus.

As a result of confusing my needs with my wants, I have wasted so much time, energy, resources, and money over the past thirty-three years. If I could take what I've misused and make good with it, my life would be positioned much more differently. Since that is not possible, I will take my experiences and teach my children a better way to maximize God's gifts to us. My prayer is for my children to discover that in addition to having a real relationship with God, food, shelter, clothing, life, health, and strength is all they really need.

> But my God shall supply all your need according to his riches in glory by Christ Jesus.
>
> Philippians 4:19 (KJV)

> I pray that God will take care of all your needs with the wonderful blessings that come from Christ Jesus!
>
> Philippians 4:19 (CEV)

After reading this timeless truth, are you confusing your wants with your needs and, in the process, squandering your time, energy, resources, and money? Are you ready to make drastic and immediate changes? Use these lines to talk to God and pray for the Holy Spirit's guidance.

_____

_____

_____

_____

_____

_____

_____

_____

_____

_____

_____

_____

_____

_____

_____

It Stinks in Here

Khalil really enjoys helping me around the house. Always welcoming the opportunity to develop new skills, he thinks it is fun to do laundry, clean his room, and cook. I truly thank God that he is embracing his self-sufficiency with pride. I want nothing more than for all of my children to develop into hard-working, responsible, independent contributors to their community and to society at large. This is the example Kenny and I attempt to model for them daily.

While preparing dinner one evening, I asked Khalil to retrieve the salmon from the deep freezer located in the garage. Upon entering, Khalil was met by a horrible stench exuding from the trash can due to be set it out for the sanitation workers to empty. With much emphasis laced with a bit of drama, Khalil shouted, "Momma, it stinks in here. Pew!" Quickly, he grabbed the salmon, came back inside the house, and shut the door. Appearing to be both offended by the odor and the task, I'm sure he wondered, *Why would she send me in there with that smell?* No one wants to be in a putrid environment.

In Isaiah chapter three, it is evident that the children of Israel have rebelled against the Lord. In verse 24 of the King James Version, we find these words:

> And it shall come to pass, [that] instead of
> sweet smell there shall be stink; and instead
> of a girdle a rent; and instead of well set hair
> baldness; and instead of a stomacher a girding
> of sackcloth; [and] burning instead of beauty.

As the body of Christ, we are supposed to exude an aroma that distinguishes us from others. In short, we are supposed to smell good. Instead, we often cause people who share our space to say, "Pew." The strife, malice, gossip, jealousy, displeasure, revenge, contempt, disrespect, resentment, anger, covetousness, and discord we often express simply do not emanate pleasantries at all. We stink. By the way, that which is not expressed—you know, the stuff we conceal in our hearts—that stinks to God.

If you will, oblige me and stop right where you are to assess your fragrance. How do you smell? Are you rosy or rotten? Don't take that question personally. Above all else, our desire should always be to grow more mature in the Lord. The only way growth can occur is when we recognize that it is necessary. So if you notice that you are giving off a foul odor, do not feel badly. If you are striving to smell good again, simply purpose in your heart that you are going to discard the garbage in your life and then follow through. I did.

> Instead of wearing seductive scents, these women are going to smell like rotting cabbages; Instead of modeling flowing gowns, they'll be sporting rags; Instead of their stylish hairdos, scruffy heads; Instead of beauty marks, scabs and scars.
>
> Isaiah 3:24 (MSG)

After reading this timeless truth, is there anything in your life you need to discard? Use these lines to talk to God and pray for the Holy Spirit's guidance and assistance.

I Don't Doubt in My Mind

My darling husband, Kenny, really needs your prayers. For as long as I've known him—which has been over nineteen years—he has been one of the most competitive people I have ever met. It does not matter what the challenge might be, Kenny is going to win, and he will make it his business to let you know he has won. While you're praying, slide one in for Kalonji as well. That lovable fruit didn't fall too far from that gung-ho tree.

We were all gathered around the kitchen table, playing one of our favorite games: "Trouble." Even though up to four people can play, Lady never ceases to charm one of us to be on our team. Who can resist a face like hers? I digress. The game begins by popping a bubble that houses a die numbered one to six. In order to leave home base, you have to pop a six. Each time you pop a six thereafter, you can take an additional piece from home base and hop around the board. The first person to get all four of their pieces back home safely is the winner.

Every player has the same chances of winning. There is no science to popping the button and no real way to determine the number that will show.

However, Kenny uses psychological scare tactics to instill fear and doubt in the minds of the other players. A few of his strategies include but certainly are not limited to:

- Looking you straight in the eyes without saying a mumbling word.

- Whispering your defeat in hopes that you will ask him, "What did you say?" to which he will say, "Oh. Nothing."

- Sympathetically pat your hand while shaking his head in a shameful manner just as you are about to pop.

- Using statements such as, "You might as well just stop playing because I've already won," or, "You better hurry up and get around that board because I'm right on your tail and I'm sending you back home."

I told you he needs prayer.

The time came for Khalil to pop. With Kenny on his heels and nearing home base, he had to be ever so careful to pop the right number. Khalil had a fifty percent chance of winning the game, which would have been his first. Right beside him, in usual manner, was Kenny, whispering sweet nothings in his ear. Khalil was cool as a cucumber. Kalonji, perplexed by his posture asked, "Khalil, you hear what Daddy is saying to you? Are you scared?" Without taking his eyes off of the board, Khalil ever so assuredly replied, "No. I'm not scared because I don't doubt it in my mind."

Khalil's words sent a bolt of electricity all throughout my body. Oh how I wish you could have been in my kitchen when he released that powerful statement from his lips. All I could shout was, "That's right, Lil." Positioned to pop, Khalil's die landed on the number he needed. He moved his final piece around the board and placed his final piece back home safely. Khalil DeBraux "the doubtless one" Parker won the game.

In June 2009, I was laid off from my job due to budget cuts. The news confirmed my desire to become a housewife once again. After being in the role for more than nine years, it was challenging at times to be gone from home for up to ten or twelve hours per day. Even though I worked in the same building where all three of my children attended school, I had lunch with them more when I was a housewife. I missed my flexible schedule and had fallen far behind in maintaining various systems. Going back home was a welcomed treat.

Five months thereafter, Kenny and I concluded that it was necessary for me to return to work. Although our day-to-day financial needs were being met—praise God, we were not living from paycheck to paycheck— and we had a growing savings account, we simply had to enhance our financial portfolio as we continued to prepare for our family's future. Additionally, we were in the process of purchasing our third home; and in order to qualify for the loan, I needed to prove employment. We sought God together through prayer and fasting and asked him to bless me with the position he wanted me to have in hopes of being a blessing to others. We kept our children abreast of what was transpiring every step of the way. As a result, Khalil, Kalonji, and Kalani prayed and fasted as well and either helped me look for jobs or encouraged me in my search.

For two months straight, I aggressively combed through Web sites and the newspaper, seeking employment. I sent out e-mails with my resume attached and text messages to family and friends informing them of my plans. Whenever I spoke to someone, I would ask that they keep me in mind, should they hear of anything. During moments of shopping for my household, I would inquire within as to whether or not a store was hiring. Most times I heard, "Not at this time." But just like Khalil, I didn't doubt it in my mind. I kept affirming, "God, I trust you, and I know you're working it out for my family." I knew God was going to keep his word and bless me with the job he wanted me to have.

Right before Christmas, we got a call from the loan officer. In no uncertain terms, he stated that our loan was being denied due to my unemployment. He then went on to say that we may qualify for a loan with another company and that my paperwork would be transferred. At this point, I went deeper into my fast and increased my job search. By the beginning of the New Year, all of the papers were signed and delivered to the new loan officer. When they received the documents, they began to verify all the information therein; and it still stated I was still employed. When I shared with them the information was not accurate, they informed me that if I did not have a job by January 18, 2010, we would be denied for the loan. Once again, that Khalil spirit swelled within me and I continued to say, "God, I trust you, and I know you're working it out for my family."

On January 10, 2010 we decided to go see the house after church. We walked in every room, marveling at how beautiful it was in its nearly complete state. The children ran to their rooms and asked me to take their pictures. Excitedly, we hurried to the basement and took in all the space we were going to have. *God, what a beautiful house,* I thought. We made our way upstairs to the main level, put on our shoes and coat, and headed outside. Just like Joshua and the children of Israel walked around the Jericho walls, we all walked round the house seven times while singing hymns.[7] Even Kalani marched in the bitter cold. Then we came back inside and gathered in the family room. I set up my camera on the kitchen bar and timed it to take a family picture. The only thing left to do was pray. We joined hands right where we were, and Kenny led us. He thanked God for blessing us with our new home, and he dedicated it back to him. He thanked God for blessing me with a job where I could be of service to him. He said that although man is trying to say, "No," God is saying, "Yes." Above all else, he prayed for the Lord's will to be done. After the final, "Amen," we got in the car and headed home.

A few days later, I sent out a prayer request to my friend Kyle in Philadelphia.

He has hosted an online prayer ministry for several years. Generally, I'm the one praying for others; but this time, it was me standing in the need of prayer. I made my request known, and Kyle sent it out to all the prayer warriors. I'm sure we number well over a hundred and fifty. A few warriors sent me e-mails with encouragement or job leads. One e-mail came from a warrior; and all she said was, "It is so." Those three words took my faith to another dimension. I can't begin to tell you the jolt that went throughout my body when I read her response. It made me say with new vitality, "God, I trust you, and I know you're working it out for my family." The next day, I had a telephone interview and was hired on the spot. The day after my telephone interview, three other employment opportunities awaited my acceptance or declination.

I have absolutely no idea what you need from God. I do know, however, that if you surrender your life to him, serve him wholeheartedly with integrity and sincerity, and never doubt that he knows what's best, his will is going to manifest in your life. Although there was a person or two who did not believe we were going to get the house and that I was not going to get a job on time, I knew that God would supply our needs. I totally trusted God and never doubted in my mind that he was working it out for my family. I implore you to follow my lead.

> *Trust in the LORD, and do good; [so] shalt thou dwell in the land, and verily thou shalt be fed.*
> Psalm 37:3 (KJV)

> God is good, a hiding place in tough times. He recognizes and welcomes anyone looking for help, No matter how desperate the trouble.
> Nahum 1:7 (MSG)

After reading this timeless truth, do you find that you doubt God more than trust God? Use these lines to talk to God. Ask him to reveal whether you are like Didymus, the Apostle who doubted that Jesus had visited the disciples, or Khalil and pray that the Holy Spirit will guide you to make all the necessary changes.[8]

_____

_____

_____

_____

_____

_____

_____

_____

_____

_____

_____

_____

_____

_____

_____

_____

Kalonji

Oh Well

October 31, 2001, at 5:44 p.m., Kalonji Ameer Parker made his grand entrée into the world. He was as plump as a Thanksgiving turkey. Weighing in at eight pounds four ounces and being twenty-one inches long, there was no doubt in mind that this child was going to be different. While I could not quite pinpoint how, something in my spirit screamed, "He is not a repeat of Khalil." Believe it or not, forty-eight hours after he was born, he rose up off of my shoulder as I was burping him. Honestly. I have a witness if you dare to challenge that statement.

In many ways, Kalonji is the mere reflection of Kenny. He is the most forthright, genuine, spontaneous, confident, unadulterated, fearless child I have ever had the pleasure of loving. Rarely is Kalonji affected by the little mishaps that he encounters. In the most unusual manner, he dismisses ill fortune quite nonchalantly.

Once, while brushing his teeth, Kalonji happened upon a nickel. He was most excited about his discovery and immediately claimed ownership. In my attempt to keep it from dropping down the drain, I moved it away from the sink. With soapy hands, Kalonji rapidly grabbed it and said, "Momma, it's my money." I attempted to explain to him that I was merely protecting the nickel; however, he was not persuaded to release the coin to me. As he prepared to rinse his hands, Kalonji dropped the nickel on the counter and turned on the water. Instead of the coin landing on its flat surface, it rolled into the bowl and began to swirl around the perimeter of the sink. Kalonji, who was more fascinated by the sight than rescuing his coin, let out a gentle, "Wow." The circling of the nickel became smaller and smaller and smaller; and finally, it went down the drain. Silence. Then, Kalonji rinsed out his mouth, turned off the water, resolved himself to what happened, and said, "Oh well."

Just as that nickel had a drain-awaited fate, in like manner is the destiny of our "possessions."

- "Wow. I cannot believe I allowed myself to get caught up in this mess. Oh well. I don't have to stay caught up. I'm coming out."

- "Wow. I thought I could confide in her, but she told just about everybody in church all my business. Oh well. I pray that my testimony, unfortunately presented in the form of gossip, draws someone closer to Christ."

- "Wow. Tell me I did not gain thirty-seven pounds in two months. Oh well. It is time to hit the gym and reinstitute a healthier diet."

- "Wow. My paycheck is gone even before I get it. Oh well. Keeping up with the Joneses has to stop. It's time I choose to save."

Today, I implore you to make a forthright, genuine, spontaneous, confident, unadulterated, fearless resolve to look at what you "own." Is it possible that you have become the COO of a situation that has totally twisted your focus? Are you in an unhealthy relationship that is keeping you from experiencing God to the fullest? Can you attest to areas of your life that really need adjusting? Is there anything that you need to drop and let go down the drain?

Please pause for a moment and ponder. It was not until I began experiencing God in ways unknown that I had the faith to lay my entire life before him and say, "Eliminate what does not belong." That request included people, projects, and plans. It is a major adjustment indeed, but all I want is what God wants for me. I do not care what he rolls down the drain because in the end, all his plans are perfect and what rolls down the drain it is really not that big of a deal.

> But seek ye first the kingdom of God, and his righteousness; and all these things shall be added unto you.
>
> Matthew 6:33 (KJV)

After reading this timeless truth, do you find that your life in more in the, "Wow," or the, "Oh well," category? Is it hard for you handle interruptions, loss, or change? Use these lines to talk to talk to God and then pray that he teach you how to seek him first.

Momma, Where Are You?

Kalonji is quite a curious child. Generally, his statements include words like *who*, *what*, *when*, *where*, *why*, and *how*. At any given moment of the day, I can expect massive interrogation on just about any subject. If I had to pinpoint the question Kalonji asks the most, it would be, "Momma, where are you?"

Whether I'm literally two feet away or two floors above him, my child will query, "Momma, where are you?" Whether he needs my assistance or no help at all, he is ready to eat or ready to sleep, he wants to be held or he desires to be left alone, he has fallen down or he is just getting up, he is playing with his toys or if parading around the house as a master drummer, Kalonji simply must ask, "Momma, where are you?"

No matter how many times a day my son seeks reassurance by asking, "Momma, where are you?" my response is always the same: "Kalonji, I'm right here. I'm right here by your side." Relating his need to know comes without challenge. Like any child desiring a sense of security and comfort from a parent, I vividly take into account asking my Parent the exact same question.

I barely want to move. Even breathing seems to be a chore. My mind is going in a quadrillion different directions and I don't have the strength to put on the brakes. Or, do I not want to? Not going to church today. Sending Kenny and the boys without me. Something's gotta be wrong for me to send my infant out of the house without me. I'm tired, angry, restless, hungry, lonely, mad, bitter, hurting, *hurting*, and all I can do is cry a river … all day long. What's happening to me? What is going on?

Stop kidding yourself, Kim. Just say it! *Just say it!* You're depressed. "I'm depressed." Depressed? Me? No way! Kimberly Kay DeBraux Parker doesn't get depressed! She moves and grooves and flows as she goes and doesn't miss a beat. She rises before the roosters and goes to bed when the owls come out and all in between she's doing just about everything under the heavens. She visits the sick and the library, prays with folk, writes to just about everyone in her phone book, shops, cooks, cleans, irons, teaches, disciplines, picks up and drops off children and dry cleaning, lays hands on and kisses little boo-boos, and she does it like a championess. What do you think this "S" on my chest stands for? Don't you see my cape flowing in the wind?

That "S" stands for "Stupid" if you think you are not going through, "Superwoman!" And you better be careful lest your cape chokes you. Could it be post partum? Nah! Kalonji is going on six months. Could it have delayed itself? That's not a nice thing to do. Not nice at all. Maybe I'm not prayed up enough. Maybe I need to read The Word more so my temple will be totally guarded from those nasty little spirits that have taken up residence on the inside. They've got to be evicted. Maybe this is just one big horrible dream and I'm about to wake up any second. Maybe not. Oh Father, where are you? God, I need to feel your presence. I need to know you're here. I need you to help me before I end up in St. E's.[9] Father, in the name of Jesus, *where are you?* Where are you ... ?[10]

That was an extremely low point in my life, quite possibly the lowest I had ever gone. I was so very broken, and all I wanted was for all of the little pieces of my life to be put back together again. I exhausted every possible option and knew that I did not have the strength to help myself. Only God was big enough to take on such a monumental task. So I cried out to the only one who was able to unravel my entangled life. As God began to reveal that he was at the center of my brokenness all along, my painful memories were being erased and a paradigm shift occurred. Every hypothesis from which I operated was silenced.

As I yielded to the mighty hand of God and allowed him to rearrange my life, he became first and foremost once more. Above all else, God wants me to be whole, sound, and of great use to him. I felt him mending me and saw the evidence of our relationship being strengthened. God was indeed the balm in my life, and the breach was finally reconstructed. Just like Joel, God compensated me for every ounce of my brokenness.[11] Whatever was lost, damaged, or stolen from me was being replaced ... with interest. Malachi 3:7 says, "Even from the days of your fathers ye are gone away from mine ordinances, and have not kept [them]. *Return unto me,* and I will *return unto* you, saith the LORD of hosts."

I was exceedingly blinded by my circumstance. With all the attention diverted on my brokenness, God seemed just so distant. However, it was only at the point of earnestly seeking him did I learn he was just a prayer away the entire time. With that realization, I eventually heard Him say to me the exact words I said to Kalonji: "I'm right here. I'm right here by your side."

> [Let your] conversation [be] without covetousness; [and be] content with such things as ye have: for he hath said, I will never leave thee, nor forsake thee.
>
> Hebrews 13:5 (KJV)

After reading this timeless truth, do you feel like you are in a broken state just as I was? Are you ready to be reconstructed? Use these lines to talk to cry out to God and then pray that he will mend every little shattered piece of your beautiful life.

_____

_____

_____

_____

_____

_____

_____

_____

_____

_____

_____

_____

_____

_____

_____

_____

You Can't See

The weather called for more snow; and that meant just one thing: hit the supermarkets and stock up. With that as my primary agenda, Kalonji and I went to four different stores and purchased all the essentials and a few tasty non-essentials too. The morning was well-spent. When we arrived home, we unloaded the groceries, put all the food away, ate a hearty lunch, and took a two-hour nap.

Upon rising, it was time to retrieve Khalil from school. After we freshened up and put on our shoes, we headed out the door. As I pulled out of my cul de sac, I realized I had forgotten my eyeglasses. Kalonji recognized the same. I knew I would be fine driving the short distance without them, so I proceeded to Khalil's school. Kalonji, on the other hand, was not so sure. In an exasperated voice, he said, "Momma, you can't see." Since he was a bit panicky, I knew he needed to be assured. The only way to do that was to provide proof. So I began pointing out cars, trees, and houses. Since I passed the sight test, he was satisfied and proceeded to relax into his car seat.

Kalonji was not the first person to utter those words to me. Several years ago, I uttered them to myself when, to my surprise, I learned I was being judgmental toward a dear friend. She claimed that whenever she would approach me for advice, my response typically left her feeling sorry she shared her issues with me in the first place. Ultimately, she would leave my presence battered and even scarred by my few choice words. In fact, there were times when all she sought was a listening ear. So, you see, I helped her none, zero, nada. At the time, I just could not see. Yet, as I revisited several conversations we had, sure enough, she was right.

Hindsight is 20/20. During such encounters, my friend was seeking sincere counsel based on truth. She wanted my opinion about what could or should be done about a situation or problem. Yet, my words came forth in the form of a subjective command laced with, "You better do…," "It's the only way…," or, "That will never work because…" I cringe even as I type those generalized statements. The doom and gloom manner in which they are presented is bound to leave anyone feeling hopeless.

Through the years, I have surmised that there is a time to speak and a time to be silent. Those who trust us enough to share deeply do not always want a response. In fact, our silence leaves room for God to speak to our hearts. He is the only one who can fix our brokenness, feelings of abandonment, and searching hearts. It is oftentimes best to state, "I am not quite sure what to say, so let us pray to God for direction." In so doing, our help will not become a hindrance.

> Judge not, and ye shall not be judged: condemn not, and ye shall not be condemned: forgive, and ye shall be forgiven.
>
> Luke 6:37 (KJV)

After reading this timeless truth, can you say you are like I once was? Have you opened your mouth one time too many and left someone feeling hopeless? Use these lines and implore God to guide you when you speak.

_____

_____

_____

_____

_____

_____

_____

_____

_____

_____

_____

_____

_____

_____

_____

I'm Not Talking to You

Kalonji has never had a problem speaking his mind. Forthright, bold, and assertive pretty much describes the way he was crafted by God. There are times when he shoots so hard from the hip that it leaves you speechless. On other occasions, his unexpected statements full of wisdom and wit confirm that he has, indeed, been here before.

One of his little friends learned this the hard way. While making our way to the movies, she felt the need to engage, uninvited, in a conversation Kalonji was having with me. Needless to say, Kalonji gave it to her straight.

"Momma? Are we there yet?" Kalonji asked.

I replied, "No, Lon. We're about two exits away."

Kalonji inquired impatiently, "What time are we gonna get there?"

"In about five minutes," I stated.

"Momma, are we at the movies now?" Kalonji asked one minute later.

His friend said, "Boy, didn't you hear what your Mother said?"

"My name is not Boy. My name is Ka-lon-ji. K-A-L-O-N-J-I," he said quite indignantly.

"Well, Ka-lon-ji, why do you keep asking the same thing?" she inquired.

Slowly turning to give her eye contact, Kalonji stated, "I'm not talking to you. I'm talking to my Momma."

That settled the conversation, for his friend said nothing more. I managed to keep my composure quite well. Slightly, I tilted the rearview mirror so they would not catch my wide-eyed expression. In a most euphemistic way, he told his friend to mind her business. Frankly, he was right. She had no right to interject in his conversation with his momma. That was between Kalonji and me.

Like you, I can name a few folks who constantly find themselves in other's business. These busy bodies never miss an opportunity to give you the 411 on someone else. With introductory conversations such as, "Chil', have you heard … ?" or, "Don't tell nobody, but … ," or, "I know I can tell *you* this … ," or, "I'm not the one to gossip, so you ain't hear this from me … ," they are always minding someone else's business.

At one point in my life, I found that I allowed myself to get swept right into those chats. As a result, I did not like the person I was becoming. So I chose to make necessary changes. Initially, my plan was to instantly remove such persons from my life; however, God had a different plan. He told me the next time someone came to me with "news," to invite her to pray for the subject of her report. Therefore, instead of talking about people, we would talk to the Lord on their behalf. Interestingly enough, when I incorporated prayer in the conversation, the calls, meetings in the ladies' room, and water cooler conversations ceased.

Prayer really does change things.

> Make it your ambition to lead a quiet life, to mind your own business …
>
> 1 Thessalonians 4:11 (NIV)

After reading this timeless truth, can you honestly say that you interject your thoughts or opinions while others are talking? Are you always in someone else's business? What do you think about such behavior? Use these lines to talk to God. Then pray that he will help you in this area.

_____

_____

_____

_____

_____

_____

_____

_____

_____

_____

_____

_____

_____

Pray and Believe

Thanksgiving Day 2009, we Parkers were on the road once more, trekking to Virginia to be with our family. We were all so very excited and looking forward to the reunion and the food aplenty. Just like any family taking a trip with children, "Are we there yet?" filled the air. The traffic was thick yet flowing steadily. We estimated our trip would take about four hours as opposed to the usual three and half hours.

Kenny and I decided to bring our laptops. Actually, it's not often that we travel without them. Kenny had intended on working on his dissertation over the break. I and the children were planning to watch movies. As we began our journey, Kalonji immediately grabbed Kenny's laptop. His mission was to play games, but the games he wanted to play were on the Internet. Since Kenny did not have an Internet card, we knew it would not be possible. However, Kalonji insisted. Moments later, we heard him exclaim, "Yes. I did it." Kalonji had found a way to play games on the Internet without an actual Internet connection.

Kenny and I were baffled for a moment. As we continued to drive, we were looking out the window to see if there were any towers nearby that would possibly aide Kalonji. After not seeing any, we all began to speculate and figured that something out there was responsible for Kalonji's sheer joy. I had to investigate. I retrieved my laptop, hoping for the same results. *This would be a great time to check all of my e-mails,* I thought. After powering up I said, "Kalonji, I believe the Web site you are on can be operated offline as well. I don't think I'll be able to get online."

Without taking his eyes off of the screen, Kalonji encouragingly replied, "Pray and believe, Momma."

Pray and believe. Pray...believe. Pray: to talk to God. Believe: to have confidence or faith in the truth. Pray and believe. They work hand in hand. They absolutely belong together like peanut butter and jelly, macaroni and cheese, fish and hot sauce, Kimberly and Kenny. In Mark 11:24, Jesus told his disciples: "Therefore I say unto you, [w]hat things so ever ye desire, when ye pray, believe that ye receive [them], and ye shall have [them]." The Message Bible puts it this way: "That's why I urge you to pray for absolutely everything, ranging from small to large. Include everything as you embrace this God-life, and you'll get God's everything."

It is impossible to pray for anything without believing we will receive what we request. So why does it occur? Quite possibly because we begin to listen to the wrong voices and tune out the voice of God. In times like this, we need to return to the Word of God and focus on what he says to us therein. The more we practice this our prayers will be met with faith instantaneously.

> So then faith [cometh] by hearing, and hearing by the word of God.
>
> Romans 10:17 (KJV)

After reading this timeless truth, is your prayer backed by your belief? Use these lines to talk to God. Then pray and believe he will respond according to his will.

_____

_____

_____

_____

_____

_____

_____

_____

_____

_____

_____

_____

_____

_____

_____

Get Up

When Khalil and Kalonji play, they engage like it is going to be their last time. *If only we could learn to live each day that way.* Watching them makes me feel like I'm at the Olympics. They run like it's the four-hundred-yard dash, jump as if hurdles meet them every ten feet, wrestle to impress the imaginary scout who is there to draft them, and make "swish" and "scoop" sounds every time their basketball goes through the net.

I clearly remember when they were much younger how Khalil and Kalonji transformed my basement on an occasion. After breakfast one cold, blustery morning, they set up various play stations from one end to the next. Although I had just done a clean sweep in the basement the day before, I knew this would keep them both quite occupied. *Great,* I thought, for it would allow me to tackle a few necessary chores around the house. As I prepared to leave, I gave them my parting speech.

"Boys?" I called.

They replied, "Yes, ma'am?"

I stated, "Please be careful down here. Don't—"

"I know, Momma. Don't jump on your couch," Khalil interrupted.

"Right, Khalil. And, please—"

"Watch out for your pictures," Khalil interjected.

Kalonji repeated, "Pictures, Momma."

I replied, "That's right, Kalonji. And I—"

Khalil interrupted once more, "Momma, I know. You don't want to hear any crying."

I started, "Good. Have—"

Before I could utter the word *fun* out of my mouth, the games had begun.

Immediately, I gathered my belongings and ascended the stairs. My goal was to maximize my time and realize at least fifty percent of my list before it was time for lunch. Round about step number eight, I heard a loud "thump" and then even louder wailing. *Oh, Lord. What happened to Khalil?* Stealthy, I crept back down a few stairs and peered through the railing. From the looks of things, Khalil had stumbled over a toy and hurt his leg. Since there was no sign of blood or broken bones, I knew he would be fine.

Kalonji, his faithful sidekick, was right by his side. I glanced at him and noticed a very peculiar look on his face. The discerner that I am, I surmised that he was trying to say something to his fallen comrade. I thought, *How sweet. Little brother desires to comfort big brother.* Consequently, I decided to observe a little longer to hear the soothing words Kalonji would share. Carefully, he knelt near his injured partner; looked directly into his eyes; wiped one tear; and said, "Get up, Khalil." Then he stood up, returned to the action figures, and continued playing. Promptly, Khalil wiped the rest of his tears and followed suit. *That's Kalonji. Nothing but tough love.*

I am most certain Khalil was hoping for a more compassionate remedy. In fact, I was just as hopeful. However, Kalonji gave him the precise medication he needed. I am inclined to believe that, had Kalonji oversympathized with Khalil, he would have stayed on the floor much longer. Indeed, a minute molehill would have become a major mountain. Since there was no blood, broken bones, or a visible sign of wounds, the only reasonable thing left for Khalil to do was, "Get up."

Getting up is a matter of choice. It is something we do from the moment we begin to crawl. This selection is made when our bodies meet the ground as we learn to ride a bike without training wheels for the first time. Time and again, we rise to the occasion and offset the opportunity to wallow in pity. Those who want the best for our lives constantly advise us to get up if at first we don't succeed. Confucius[12] said, "Our greatest glory is not in never falling, but in rising every time we fall."[13]

Please take this page out of a day in the life of Khalil and Kalonji. Maybe you have found yourself at a crossroad and you think starting over is impossible. Well, it is not. You can get up. The mistake you made is not as big as you think, so don't let the war going on inside of your mind and the stigma keep you down. Get up. The predicament in which you find yourself is by far not unique. It has occurred in the life of someone else before and they survived. Do you not know that you will survive, too? Get up.

Just as Kalonji was by his brother's side, aiding him in his time of need, God is right by your side, waiting to aide you. He said most clearly in Psalm 46:1, "God [is] our refuge and strength, a *very present help* in trouble." Do you understand what that means? Literally, this passage is saying:

> The one Supreme Being, creator, and ruler of the universe exists for us as shelter, protection, power, authority, and an extreme and immedi-

ate contributor of assistance during unfortunate or distressing circumstances.

I do believe that says it all. The only thing left for you to do at this point is, "Get up."

> God-loyal people don't stay down long; Soon they're up on their feet, while the wicked end up flat on their faces.
>
> Proverbs 24:16 (MSG)

After reading this timeless truth, can you identify with Khalil? Have you fallen and can't get up? Do you want to stay there or rise once more? Use these lines to talk to God. Then pray that he will send a Kalonji-type your way to help you in this area.

_____

_____

_____

_____

_____

_____

_____

_____

_____

_____

_____

_____

_____

_____

That's My Brother

Elation, gratitude, anticipation—these are just a few words I would use to describe how I felt when Saturday finally arrived and I had nothing scheduled outside of the house. After working up to ten hours per day, attending evening meetings, facilitating workshops, and shuffling the children back and forth to various extracurricular activities the five days prior, zilch one day out of the week truly made my hallelujah chorus croon. To my most pleasant surprise, Khalil and Kalonji did not barrage me with such questions like, "Momma, where are we going today? Can you take us to the park? Are we able to ride our bikes in the cul de sac? Do you want to go visit Aunt Kim?"

Apparently, they were just as ready to relax as I was.

Since the order for the day was freedom and flexibility, I allowed them to do whatever they desired as long as they put in their daily required reading of thirty minutes and completed their chores. Video games, action figures, cards, board games, television, coloring, puzzles, ripping and running, and wrestling were permitted. They deserved that break because the next day would jumpstart our week destined to be full of activity once more.

Making my way downstairs with a load of laundry, I found the boys comfortably lying on the living room floor. They were engaged in one of their most favorite activities: coloring.

Kalonji noticed Khalil's progress and said, "That looks nice, Khalil. You color good inside the lines." Kalonji studied Khalil's pattern a little longer and then looked at me and said, "Momma, that's my brother."

A chill went down my spine as he uttered that statement laced with pride, protection, and humility.

I will be the first to admit that Kalonji is not the gooey type. And while I have yet to witness him become extremely sentimental or overflow with emotions that do not stem from any personal experiences, of this one thing I am certain: he really admires Khalil and has asserted himself as his essential minder. Yes, they have their typical sibling issues; but when it comes right down to it, I pity the person who attempts to cross Khalil in Kalonji's presence.

One such incident is forever embedded in my psyche. Khalil and Kalonji were outside playing basketball with a child in our neighborhood. A tough little boy with a very strong will, he began to engage unfairly by keeping control of the ball beyond the allotted time. Khalil, who generally tries to keep peace, did not assert himself. When I spoke to him later, he explained that he knew he would get the ball eventually. Kalonji, on the other hand, was not interested in the long run. So he went over to the little boy; stood firmly in front of him; and said, "That's not fair. It's Khalil's turn, man. Give him the ball." Without hesitation, the little boy passed the ball to Khalil and the game continued the right way.

Many are the questions contained within the Word of God. If I had to pinpoint one that resonates as a result of this experience it is found in Genesis 4:9: "Am I my brother's keeper?" This familiar passage reflecting brotherly love and mutual respect to the contrary strikes at the heart of the matter and should propel everyone reading this entry to reply with a reverberating, "Yes, I am." Biological ties matter not, for we all need someone to concern themselves with our well being and vice versa. Jesus charged all of us with having the best interest of someone else in mind when he said, "Thou shalt love thy neighbour as thyself."[14]

Thank you, Kalonji, for demonstrating in both word and deed that Khalil is indeed your brother and you, unwaveringly so, are Khalil's keeper.

The commandments, Do not commit adultery, Do not murder, Do not steal, Do not covet, and whatever other commandment there may be, are summed up in this one rule: Love your neighbor as yourself.

Romans 13:9 (NIV)

After reading this timeless truth, whom would you say is your neighbor? What are you doing to be someone's keeper? Use these lines to talk to God. Then pray that your relationships will continue to flourish.

_____

_____

_____

_____

_____

_____

_____

_____

_____

_____

_____

_____

_____

_____

_____

Kalani

I'm Blessed

Every now and again, I tune into the "Enduring Truth" broadcast with Pastor Paul Sheppard. If I do not catch him at home on my radio, I log onto his Web site and tap into his free podcast. Pastor Sheppard has a very unique style of incorporating humor with real-life examples of how to walk this Christian walk. The truth that emanates over the airways has aided in my spiritual transformation.

Kalani, who shadows me around the house, was in my bedroom, playing with her doll. My moving about and Pastor Sheppard's fiery sermon did not distract her from her "motherly" duties of dressing, grooming, and feeding her "baby." At the conclusion of the broadcast, Pastor Sheppard asked his listening audience a very poignant question: "Are you blessed today?" Out of nowhere; Kalani went over to the radio; raised her hand and said, "Yes. I'm blessed today."

As I looked at my daughter intently trying to prove her point to Pastor Sheppard, I quietly said, "I know exactly what you mean, Lady."

I have countless stories that truly illustrate just how blessed I am. Whether emotional, spiritual, physical, material, or financial, my cup truly overflows. My most recent blessing is one that is head and shoulders above the rest. While shopping for a suit, I remembered that I needed another skirt for my wardrobe as well. An hour was already well-spent searching and trying on several items of clothes, so I was not interested in investing too much time in the pursuit of a skirt.

I walked directly to the skirt rack, flipped through a handful, and found one with a $5.00 price tag. It was black with lining and the only one left. I was thrilled. I'm a very frugal person and take great pride in finding a bargain. Quitting while I was ahead, I skipped to the check-out line and laid my items on the counter. When Sharon, the cashier, scanned the skirt, the register beeped twice as if to say, "No-no"; and then it happened. "Ramon, I need a price check, please." Sharon called the manager because there appeared to be something wrong with the $5.00 price of the skirt.

I chuckled a bit because whenever I'm shopping and it's time for me to pay for my items, the cashier either needs a price check or runs out of register tape. I know that's God's design simply to help me in the area of patience. As I waited for Ramon, above a whisper, I humbly said, "God, I'd really like this skirt for five dollars." I've learned over the years that it is important to be specific with God. Although he already knows what we need, the power of our words aids the manifestation process.

Ramon approached the counter and greeted me cordially. Sharon scanned the item for him. When he heard the double beep, he put his key in the register, typed in a code, and the register beeped twice again.

I asked him if there was a problem with the skirt; and he replied, "It's not ringing up for five dollars. It's saying twenty-one ninety-nine. Do you still want it?"

I politely said, "I sure do, sir, but for five dollars."

He smiled and turned to Sharon and said, "I need to go check this out."

About seven minutes passed before Ramon returned. He beckoned Sharon to him and whispered something in her ear.

She returned to the register; looked at me; and stated, "Today is your lucky day. He told me to ring the skirt up for one cent."

That's right. The twenty-two-dollar skirt was reduced all the way down to a penny.

Before I knew it, I told Sharon, "It's not luck, Sharon. I'm blessed."

With a puzzled look on her face, Sharon handed me my bag and said, "Well, you better hurry up and run out of this store before he changes his mind."

As I retrieved my merchandise, I thanked Sharon for her service; asked her to thank Ramon for the discount; and confidently said, "When you have the favor of God on your life, the only running you do is to go tell it."

> So shalt thou find favour and good understanding in the sight of God and man.
>
> Proverbs 3:4 (KJV)

After reading this timeless truth, do you recognize that you are blessed? Use these lines to list all of the blessings God has bestowed upon you and thank him for being so loving, gracious, and caring.

_____

_____

_____

_____

_____

_____

_____

_____

_____

_____

_____

_____

_____

_____

_____

_____

Did He Die For Jesus?

All week long, I looked forward to this moment. The neglect was more than I could stomach, and my longing became unbearable. The extensive lack of connection fostered the need for a reunion. Enough was really enough. Day after day, I would peer through my kitchen window and pray for just a little time, a little time to rake leaves and clean the debris in my backyard.

I dare not bore you with my schedule. It is probably safe to say that you do not desire to hear me belt out lyrics detailing what it takes to manage a five-person household (six when Bricen visits) on a daily basis. So please just trust me when I tell you that "The Chauffeur in Me," "Fifteen Loads of Laundry," "Soccer Mom Medley," and "Clean Your Plate ... and the Other Dishes Too" have all topped the music charts in the palace for years. So you see an early morning rendezvous with nature was a welcomed break from the norm.

What began as a solo project (which is always my preference when I am on a schedule), evolved into a duet most immediately. My "green" baby, Kalani, was so full of life as she marched through the grass and into the open backyard. Nearly five months prior, we had all of our trees removed; so Kalani had her run of the place. There she was in her faded pink corduroy pants settling way above her ankles and revealing her purple socks, beige down coat, multi-colored rain hat, pink-and-white cat-face rain boots, and her pink sunglasses. It was obvious she dressed herself. Fashion faux pas aside, Kalani was ready to work in the yard with her momma.

After giving me a hug and a big kiss, she reached for the little hoe and began to dig. Just as I was returning to bag more leaves, Kalani screamed, "Momma! Momma! Come look. Quickly!"

Now, surprising as this might be, I don't like to be too close to nature, let alone its inhabitants. Yes, I wanted to be as one with the leaves; but not in a dive-and-roll-around-in-them kind of way. My goal was simply to remove them off the floor of my yard. That's all.

Ever so cautiously, I walked to where my three-year-old was kneeling down. She kept poking at the ground with the little hoe and rather insistently said, "Look, Momma. See dat?"

When I told her all I saw was dirt, a stick, and pebbles, she replied, "Dat's not a stick, Momma. Dat's a worm."

Sure enough, it was a worm that just so happened to be dead. Not a problem for Kalani, of course, who retrieved the carcass with her bare hands and dangled it in front of her face. Oh yuck.

Thoroughly, she inspected the worm. She appeared to be a bit bewildered; so I asked her, "What's wrong, Lady?"

"Momma," she said, "da worm not moving. I want da worm to move, Momma."

Having arrived on the scene when I did, I had very little detail of the worms' expiration. Was it an accidental homicide as a result of Kalani poking around with the hoe? Did a bird, within its rights in the circle of life, briefly encounter its appetizer with plans to return? Or had nature merely taken her course and the worm's clock just stopped ticking?

Unsure of the particulars, I gently replied, "Lady, the worm is dead."

For about thirty seconds more, Kalani held the worm near her eyes. She gently shook it and faintly whispered, "Move, worm." Realizing her best efforts yielded the same response, she knelt back down and carefully placed the worm on a multicolored leaf.

As it laid there, a story about that worm's season in life unfolded. The green hue in the leaf represented its birth. The reddish-orange splash represented the stages of its life. The brown tint represented its death.

As Kalani stood to her feet, she looked at me and asked, "Momma, did he die for Jesus?"

Totally shocked by her inquiry, I gently stroked her arm; smiled; and said, "Lady, I sure hope he did."

Kalani's innocent inquiry forced me to ask myself an even greater question: Am I living for Jesus? Does my walk mirror Christ? Do I invest enough time in studying his Word? Do I consistently testify of his saving power? Is my non-verbal witness exemplifying total obedience to the Holy Scriptures? How I live is of greater importance, for it determines how I die. There in the dash resting between the year I was born and the year I expire laid the answer to my question.

Exploring my annals, that dash revealed that I did not consistently live for Jesus. For an extensive period of time, he was not the head of my life. I lived on my own terms or allowed myself to be persuaded by others, thus living on their terms. Going to the club outnumbered going to church, and the company I kept generally left me in far too many compromising situations that could have easily been the death of me. I did not honor my parents the way God commanded because I was too engrossed in the pain I accused them of causing. I was literally walking dead, barely living for myself, let alone Jesus.

Years have now come and gone since then. Far be it for me to say that I have arrived; however, I am on God's side now and strive to live for Jesus daily. Just as Paul said:

> Brethren, I count not myself to have appre-hended: but [this] one thing [I do], forgetting those things which are behind, and reach-ing forth unto those things which are before, I press toward the mark for the prize of the high calling of God in Christ Jesus.[15]

I have become more aware of what I must do to fol-low him and serve others. Through prayer, fasting, and studying the Bible, I strengthen my relationship with him and add to my testimony. I continuously seek God and ask him to reveal unto me those areas of my life that prevent me from effectively serving him and others. I pray to be shown practical ways to be a blessing to others. Because I am equipped with the power of God to make changes in my life, each day God perfects me, making me over in ways too numerous to name.

Am I living for Jesus? Oh yes. More now than ever before.

> For to me to live [is] Christ, and to die [is] gain.
>
> Philippians 1:21 (KJV)

After reading this timeless truth, can you say assuredly that you are living for Jesus? What would others say? Use these lines to talk to God and pray to be shown how to live for him more and more each day.

Out of the Mouths of Babes

_____

_____

_____

_____

_____

_____

_____

_____

_____

_____

_____

_____

_____

_____

I Can't Hear That

The more I engage with Kalani, the more astounded I am by her honesty, humility, and intellect. Never one to mince her words, she uninhibitedly speaks directly from a place of emotion. Her capacity for learning, reasoning, and understanding and her aptitude in grasping truths surfaces at the most unexpected moments. In short, she is a very bold, bright, and sincere child.

While leaving Bible study one Wednesday night, Sister Phyllis, who normally rides home with us, began conversing about the stages in the relationship between a man and a woman. Casually, we discussed the transition from being single to being a couple. I even shared a few precious details of my courtship to Kenny. Realizing Kalani was with us, we trod that delicate ground ever so cautiously and made sure that we chose our words deliberately. As we continued chatting, Sister Phyllis used the words *girlfriend* and *boyfriend* in her sentence.

Before she could put a period at the end of her sentence, Kalani gently stated, "Sista Phyllis, I can't hear that."

Sister Phyllis paused for about ten seconds. She looked at Kalani, who was sitting next to her, and then at me through my rearview mirror. With a frozen look of shock on her face, she asked, "Did she just say what I think she said?"

Straightway, Kalani stopped playing with her doll; looked directly as Sister Phyllis; interjected; and replied, "I can't hear that word because I'm too little."

"Oh. I apologize, Lady. I will not say that word again," Sister Phyllis replied most respectfully.

During my quiet time later that evening, I marveled at my daughter's statement and began thinking about all the conversations I allow in my presence, particularly those that I engage in with myself. Sitting there alone and in silence, I became extremely fixated on how entangled I become with my inner me. The motion picture movie playing inside my head engulfs me to the point where I just cannot shake loose what's going on between my ears. The only way the curtain calls and credits begin to roll is when I begin talking out loud to myself.

Not long ago, I had one such tête-à-tête. After a week-long "State of Kimberly" forum that left me anxious, condemned, doubtful, fretting, and fearful, I came to this conclusion as recorded in my spiritual journal:

Just the other day, I said to myself, "Self?" and myself said, "Hum?" and I said, "You need to start speaking and proclaiming the promises of God over your life!" As God would have it, I just read 2 Peter 1:4 where it says, "Whereby are given unto us exceeding great and precious promises; that by these ye might be partakers of the divine nature, having escaped the corruption that is in the world through lust." The Message puts it this way: "We were also given absolutely terrific promises to pass on to you—your tickets to participation in the life of God after you turned your back on a world corrupted by lust."[16] Promises. God takes them seriously and it's high-time I do the same! The more I hear them ringing in my head, the less I'll hear defeat, disappointment, and devastation. Believe in the power and promises of the blood so not to further persecute Jesus, the Christ![17]

Kalani knew and adequately expressed that the word *boyfriend* was not to be spoken in her presence. She did what she had to do to guard her innocence and would not tolerate the tainting of her temple with such unsuitable language. In essence, Kalani protected herself because Kalani valued herself. What an important lesson to learn from a four-year-old. Thank you, Kalani, for being such a valuable example to your momma.

> For all the *promises* of God in him [are] yea, and in him Amen, unto the glory of God by us.
> 1 Corinthians 1:20 (KJV)

After reading this timeless truth, do you believe you entertain unwholesome conversations? Do you allow people to speak negativity in your presence? Use these lines to talk to God and listen clearly to what he has to say about this matter.

_____

_____

_____

_____

_____

_____

_____

_____

_____

_____

_____

_____

_____

_____

It's Gonna Be a Great Day

It is often a struggle to get my children up in the morning. Nestled ever so warmly in their blankets, resolutely, they contend with the task of disconnecting themselves from their beds. With crust in eyes and dried saliva trailing down the side of their lovely faces, they faintly whisper, "Just five more minutes, Momma."

On one such occasion, Kalani decided to forego the extra time and popped right up. She stood up tall, stretched her arms and legs, and let out her morning yawn. After greeting me with a most precious, "Good Morning, Momma," she grabbed my legs and squeezed them as tight as her little arms could. Kalani was vibrant and ready to take on the day. Noticing her brothers were still in the bed, she tipped over to them and stated, "Get up because it's gonna be a great day." Those choice words lit a spark in me; and five minutes later, this affirmation was born:

> I am on my way but wanted to say …
> It's gonna be a great day!
> When I get to school I will fol-
> low the rules …
> It's gonna be a great day!

I'll have fun and share; be
nice and play fair …
It's gonna be a great day!
I will do my work and pay attention
and keep myself out of detention …
It's gonna be a great day!
Applied knowledge is power! I'll
get smarter by the hour …
It's gonna be a great day!
I won't hang with bad crowds because
I want to make my family proud …
It's gonna be a great day!
I will help who I can and
lend them a hand …
It's gonna be a great day!
When my school day is through,
I'll know what to do …
It's gonna be a great day!
Walk in pairs or ride the bus and
will not shout, scream, or fuss …
It's gonna be a great day!
My homework will be done completely; I will
check my answers and write quite neatly …
It's gonna be a great day!
While eating with my family, we will
talk to each other honestly …
It's gonna be a great day!

After dinner, I will help maintain
the cleanliness of our domain …
It's gonna be a great day!
Wash my body and brush my teeth
from left to right, for my busy
day has turned to night …
It's gonna be a great day!
Time to end my day this way: be-
fore I sleep, I have to pray …
Thank you, God! It really was a great day!

[It is of] the LORD's mercies that we are not
consumed, because his compassions fail not.
[They are] new every morning: great [is] thy
faithfulness.

Lamentations 3:22–23 (KJV)

After reading this timeless truth, are you determined
to make your day great no matter what comes your
way? Use these lines to talk to God and praise him in
advance for having a great day.

_____

_____

_____

_____

_____

_____

_____

_____

_____

_____

_____

_____

_____

_____

Cast Your Cares

It was simply one of those weeks. My failures over the past six days gladly made my acquaintance with the morning light and not-so-gently prepared me for slumber at night. Unlike a few years ago, I grasped the magnitude of prayer and fasting, totally embraced its relevance, and regularly incorporated it into my life. It's common place for me to wake up and say, "Three days; liquids only; no TV," or implement another fast that will increase my strength, clean my heart, and renew my mind. However, no matter how much I prayed and affirmed positivity out loud I truly could not shake myself loose.

In an attempt to shift my thinking, I immersed myself into many loads of laundry. Of course, my little lady, Kalani, was right by my side, lending a helping hand. She always looks forward to folding the towels and washcloths. Her task is not complete unless she shows me each one and places it in the linen closet one at a time. Sometimes, she makes up to twenty trips; but I never try to usurp her system. If it ain't broke, don't fix it, right?

Making her way back to the boy's room to retrieve the last few items, I noticed she was mumbling. I did not interrupt her conversation, for the one going on inside my head took precedence. With her lips still moving, Kalani folded another towel and carried it to the linen closet just as she had done all the others. But when she came back into the room, this time, she tapped me on my leg; looked me square in the eyes; and said most assuredly, "Momma, remember: 'Cast your cares on the Lord.'"[18] Her words froze me in place. *How on earth did she know I was burdened?* I thought. I wondered, *Did my body language utter words of frustration? Was I unusually firm with the laundry? Did I have an atypical expression on my face?* However Kalani gleaned my unrest, her summation was accurate and her solution was even more precise.

Surely I was getting a taste of my own medicine. Not only was it the scripture Kalani shared in front of the church on Youth Sunday, but 1 Peter 5:7 is one of the passages that I have hid in my heart[19] and pull upon to encourage myself and my children. Quite frankly, this scripture saved my marriage. I'll reserve that information for now and possibly share it in the third edition of this book.

After Kalani's sermon, I gave her a really big hug. I don't think she'll ever know just how much she blessed me with her simplicity. While my departure from Burdenville was not immediate, Kalani helped me begin to navigate myself away from my troubled thoughts. I realized that success and failure is a matter of perspective and that each day is filled with both. It is a matter of choice which one I choose to dominate my psyche. Besides, what I deem as a setback could ultimately be God setting me up for comeback. His thoughts and his ways are not the same as mine because he sees so much more than I ever will.[20]

Thank you, Lord! Thank you, Kalani!

> Casting the whole of your care [all your anxieties, all your worries, all your concerns, once and for all] on Him, for He cares for you affectionately and cares about you watchfully.
>
> 1 Peter 5:7 (TAB)

After reading this timeless truth, do you think you've been casting your cares on the Lord or concealing your cares in your heart? Do you want peace of mind? Use these lines to talk to God and listen clearly to what he has to say about this matter.

_____

_____

_____

_____

_____

_____

_____

_____

_____

_____

_____

_____

_____

_____

_____

Say Yes or No

It was Christmas Day 2009, and I rose bright and early to continue working on this book. Before I got out of the bed, I prayed and asked God to inspire me from the moment I began typing until I placed a final period at the end of a sentence. With Kenny and boys already in Norfolk and Kalani still asleep, the house was serene. I anticipated accomplishing a great deal of work.

I was making great strides. As I worked on the chapter about Khalil, God showed me that this book would serve as a journal for my readers. He led me to add a page after each entry whereby you can share your thoughts and feelings too. I know how important it is to release bottled up emotions. For years, my journal was the only "person" with which I shared my joys and pains. I pray the few lines I've left for you serve its purpose well.

Preparing to move on to the next entry, a knock came at the office door. I paused my typing in hopes that it was just my imagination running away with me. Then there was more knocking. Hesitantly, I opened the door. There stood Kalani. My little lady had risen and was ready to take on the day. Immediately following, "Good Morning, Momma," she made her request known.

"Momma, may I please watch the TV?" she asked.

I replied, "Maybe. After you have eaten breakfast."

"I don't understand," she said puzzling.

"What don't you understand, Lady?" I inquired.

"I don't understand, 'maybe,' Momma. Can't you say yes or no? Just pick one, Momma," she requested.

Then an awkward silence filled the room. You know: the hush that sweeps in when you just do not know what to say. The deafening sound of nothing, stillness even, enveloped both Kalani and I as she waited for my response. Challenged by her question, I felt trapped, backed into a corner. To answer her meant that I would have to make a decision and come down off of the fence I had straddled. That fence keeps me from saying what I desire not to for one reason or another. "No" was my answer of choice because she had already exceeded her television limits for the week. However, "no," based on past experiences, would have evoked pouting and cascading tears.

As uncomfortable as my predicament was, Kalani was absolutely correct. My four-year-old daughter was encouraging me to say what I mean and mean what I say. Editing my words according to what I think she can handle does not serve either of us well.

If Kalani does not learn to deal with no from me, then she is in for a rude awakening when she encounters it outside the safe haven of her home.

Unwavering, I turned to Kalani and simply stated, "No." Once again, a long hush overcame us both as we stared at each other.

With a partially shocked expression on her most adorable face, she said, "But you said, 'maybe,' Momma."

Suppressing my laughter, I replied, "Well, I took your advice, and now I'm saying no."

Kalani took a deep sigh. As she was exiting the office, she turned back, looked at me, and said, "Okay, Momma." Then she walked into the family room where she proceeded to play in her kitchen.

Passive aggressive communication, waffling, or hinting really does a disservice to both you and the recipient. This type of dialogue can be misleading and disingenuous. Though awkward and even difficult at best, in the end it is always best to say what needs to be said with assurance. In so doing, we remain true to ourselves and trustworthy to others.

But let your communication be, Yea, yea; Nay, nay: for whatsoever is more than these cometh of evil.

Matthew 5:37 (KJV)

Let your Yes be simply Yes, and your No be simply No; anything more than that comes from the evil one.

Matthew 5:37 (TAB)

Just say "yes" and "no." When you manipulate words to get your own way, you go wrong.

Matthew 5:37 (MSG)

After reading this timeless truth, do you say what you mean and mean what you say? Use these lines to talk to God and pray for him to help you speak confidently.

_____

_____

_____

_____

_____

_____

_____

_____

_____

_____

_____

_____

_____

_____

_____

_____

The "G" Word

Kalani and I found ourselves, once again, engaged in playing cat and mouse. I get a kick out of watching her round the corner of the sofa as she attempts to catch me. Sometimes, I let her get right on my heels and then I put my stride in fifth gear and I'm off. Nothing but smoke trails from me as my stomach aches from laughing.

After running through the house and escaping her little clutches for about twenty minutes, I decided to pump my brakes without warning. Kalani, who had taken her eyes off of me for a few seconds, crashed right into my thigh, bounced back, and landed smack on her derrière. We were both rolling over with laughter or ROWL. That's text language in case you did not know.

After finally composing ourselves, I helped Kalani off the floor and we headed to the bathroom to wash our hands in preparation for snack time. Homemade popcorn with sea salt, sliced red delicious apples, and juice was on the menu that day. After everything was prepared, we sat at the kitchen table and began to relive the fun we just had

"Momma, we had fun, didn't we?" Kalani asked.

I replied, "We sure did."

Kalani stated, "You're real funny too, Momma."

"Girl, you are funnier than I am," I retorted.

Instantly, Kalani stopped what she was doing and looked me straight in the eyes. The unfamiliar blank expression on her face concerned me. *Was she choking on the apple and was not able to breathe?* I thought. Then I remembered what I learned in CPR about choking: Kalani, more than likely, would have been clutching her throat. Still, I could not understand why she was so frozen.

A few seconds later, Kalani said, "Momma, you called me the 'G' word. I am not 'girl.' I'm Lady."

The "G" word? I thought. *What does a three-year-old child know about the "G" word?* I pondered. I chuckled as I sat looking at this beautiful gift God obviously felt I was fit to love, train, and nurture. On the outside, she stood less than three feet tall; but on the inside, she was a giant. Kalani knew who she was and was not going to let anyone, not even her Momma, tell her otherwise. What took her three years to embrace took me thirty years to embrace.

The Bible entails countless statements that clearly reveal who we are in Christ:

We are a new creation! (2 Corinthians 5:17)

We are children of God! (John 1:12)

We are a royal priesthood! (1 Peter 2:9)

We are the salt of the earth! (Matthew 5:13)

We are children of the light! (1 Thessalonians 5:5)

With that, I have just one question to ask: Who are you?

> For we are his workmanship, created in Christ Jesus unto good works, which God hath before ordained that we should walk in them.
>
> Ephesians 2:10

After reading this timeless truth, can you honestly say you know who you are? Use these lines to talk to God and pray for him to help you recognize your true self-worth.

_____

_____

_____

_____

_____

_____

_____

_____

_____

_____

_____

_____

_____

_____

_____

Notes

Khalil

1. "Wikipedia.com: The Free Encyclopedia." 18 December 2009 <http://en.wikipedia.org/wiki/Kids_Say_the_Darndest_Things/>

2. Tapping the Power Within: A Path to Self-Empowerment for Black Women. Copyright © 1992 Iyanla Vanzant Writers and Readers Publishing.

3. Eastern Community Church is located in Landover, MD. Rev. Damion M. Briggs is the Pastor. <http://easterncommunity.org>

4. Judges 6:37–40

5. Journal Entry. July 4, 1994, 10:33am

6. Joseph Medlicott Scriven, (September 10, 1819–August 10, 1886) was an Irish poet. He wrote a poem to comfort his mother called "Pray Without Ceasing." It was later set to music and renamed by Charles C. Converse, a United States attorney who also worked as a composer of church songs, becoming the hymn "What a Friend We Have in Jesus." "Wikipedia.org." 26 December 2009 <http://en.wikipedia.org/wiki/Joseph_Scriven>

7. Joshua 6

8. John 20

Kalonji

9. St. Elizabeth's Hospital is a psychiatric hospital in Washington, DC. Formerly called the Government

Hospital for the Insane, St. E's, as it is referred to, was declared a National Historic Landmark in 1991.

10. Journal Entry. April 28, 2002, 8:37am.

11. Joel 2:25–26

12. Confucius (551–479 BCE), according to Chinese tradition, was a thinker, political figure, educator, and founder of the *Ru* School of Chinese thought. "Stanford Encyclopedia of Philosophy Online." 2006. Stanford University. 5 September 2006 <http://plato. stanford.edu/entries/confucius/>

13. "Proverbia.net." 2009. Famous Quotes, Quotations, and Proverbs. <http://en.proverbia.net/citasautor. asp?autor=11645/>

14. Matthew 22:39

Kalani

15. Philippians 3:13, 14

16. Eugene H. Peterson, The Message Bible

17. November 22, 2009 at 6:59am

18. 1 Peter 5:7

19. Psalms 119:11

20. Isaiah 55:8